W9-APH-921

Table of Contents

Preface

In a person's life, there is at least one point that he 'stops his life' because he has questions about the meaning of life. The answers might be found in religious or traditional ways of life, or by getting professional help, like from a psychiatrist. It could also be advice from other people. In the worst of cases, he's left without answers, and continues his life with unanswered questions. When we were kids, we just could ask questions our parents or our teacher and got the answers. As an adult the questions about life become more complicated and the answers as well. Most of the times, it's hard to find the right answer. When a person gets into a crisis situation and/or gets into chronic feelings of confusion, desperation or helplessness, the questions about life become urgent, complicated and life-changing.

I was at this point. It came because of a crisis: I hit rock bottom. I lost my way in life and no hope was in the horizon. I felt helpless and was looking for answers about my way in life. I tried the possibilities mentioned above, all of them, but the answers weren't enough. I felt the emptiness; it was like a black hole that sucked me in. I was there for a while.

Until, in a moment of inspiration, I gathered myself and made a decision that caused a deep change in my life: to start a life journey in order to find my truth of life. I knew the truth had to be somewhere and I just had to look for it.

I found myself moving forward in a journey to the spiritual world. I'd heard before about the spiritual world but I didn't believe in it back then. But with my motivation to find answers, I decided to try it by myself.

On my journey to the spiritual world I participated in workshops, went to festivals, read books, got treatment from alternative caregivers, went to lectures, joined communities, studied how to do alternative treatments, and after much practice, I began to use energy treatments in my own clinic. I had goals to achieve along the journey, which motivated me to continue moving forward and to be focused and I knew that one day I would get all the answers that I needed, and this day finally came.

While moving forward on my journey, I noticed that although the spiritual world --typically characterized as metaphysical, abstract, endless and undefined-- was different from what I thought it would be before getting into it. Looking at the big picture, I realized that the spiritual world has patterns and rules. As a researcher, I wanted to take a closer look at these characteristics. Therefore, during my journey I found myself using my professional skills to explore and analyze the spiritual world by using a systematic process of mapping and coding. I used a consistent process of Scientific Modeling[1] for a wide variety of informal methods: ways of life, workshops, mantras, treatments, beliefs and even principles from the Old and New Testaments.

The motivation to develop the model became stronger after I got deeper into the spiritual world but at the same time disconnected from the material world. It seemed that life was splitting into two separate worlds: the material world and the spiritual world. For that reason, I wanted to find the bridge between these two worlds. The model was the ultimate tool to do it: to validate the aspects of the spiritual world in reality by using scientific tools (as much as I

---

[1] In www.FindMagicLife.com you can find details on the process of developing the model.

could), and make the knowledge of the spiritual world practical in the material world.

Another purpose of the model was its ability to spread the word: I was so excited from finding the spiritual world that I wanted to tell to the world: "Listen! There is another way to live life!" I knew that people (back then 'people' were my close circle but over the years I've expanded the circle) would understand me only if I translated the wisdom of the spiritual world to tangibility. In other words, to expose the secrets of the spiritual world for every person that wants to live full life.

The outcome of the modeling process is the 'Poles Inversion' model that this book is based on.   The 'Poles Inversion' means changing one's attitude about the relationship he has with his reality: instead of just responding to reality, the person creates his own reality. It's a truth that we've forgotten. The model shows and proves that there is a way a person can control his life, which means to have the freedom to live his life according to his wishes.

The book will be your personal guide and show you the way to your life journey, which you can follow to fulfill your goals in your life.

Introduction

The purpose of this book is to lay out a guide for life, based on a logical model that I've been developing for the past few years.
I developed the model in order to make the spiritual world accessible and also practical for every person. In other words, I was looking for the bridge between the spiritual world and the material world. It has been my life project for the last 7 years and I've enjoyed every moment of it.

The modeling of the spiritual world was a process of mapping, coding and analyzing a world that's beyond our logical comprehension. To achieve this, I used a special technique that's based on scientific tools to develop the model and also validate it in reality.
The outcome is 'Poles Inversion': a reliable, proofed and validated model that explains the processes and rules in our world beyond, which means the mysterious, magical, and unexplainable.

This book is a guide for a life journey according to the principles of the Poles Inversion Model.
It can be your journey: to find the magic in your life and use it to fulfill your wishes.
The starting point will be your life at the present time. Then, after a decision has been made about what your goals are, the guide will lead you to navigate your life to fulfill them.

During the journey, you will sharpen and clarify your decisions; use fears to motivate and to navigate; empower your faith in yourself in order to be consistent on your path; harness your passion in order to generate your motivation to move forward through barriers; discover your vision about your life; empower your self-belief; focus your skills and abilities on whatever task you have at hand; and learn and practice being the creator of your life.

As you work through your life according to the guidance of this book, you will soon realize that it is only you who creates the reality of your life; it's all according to your decisions.

For maximum results, the book includes a series of step-by-step practical tools that you can implement at any moment in your life.

You can start the journey now. Shall we begin?

How to use this book

At every point in your life, you have goals to fulfill. Sometimes you know what the specific goal is and sometimes you only know that you need a change.

Goals like career change, losing weight, exercise endurance, improving health, improving the quality of your life, personal achievement, empowering family relationships, finding a significant other, empowering social relationships – they are all meaningful and require changes in habits, changes in your way of life.

You will make a decision to fulfill a personal goal and this book will be your guide. Think of it as if you were walking on a path towards your goal and the Guide is like a GPS, pointing you in the right direction at every step.

This Guide has been presented to you in a workshop format that includes procedural instructions, a step-by-step guide.

To get the most out of this Guide, do one step at a time. Apply each when you are alone, located in an inspiring environment for you (on the beach, at the park, in a coffee shop, quiet place in your house, etc.).

The key here is acceptance and diligence. Accept the process as it is, just follow the words and they will take you to the exact place you need to be.

Negative attitudes like resistance, doubts, criticism or cynicism are part of the process, don't worry about them, just accept them and continue with the steps in the Guide. It will all become clear during the process.

Prepare a new notebook and pen. Even if you'd normally use a screen, it's strongly recommended that you use traditional pen and paper for this creative process.

Are you ready?

Chapter 1:
Change begins from the inside

To make a change in your life, you have to begin on the inside, which means from your inner world. Therefore, this book will guide you first to make the change in your inner world, and then in your reality.

Let's begin with understanding what we have under the hood: what does your inner world include?

Your inner world: thoughts, feelings, deep essence

Your inner world includes 3 layers: thoughts, feelings, and deep essence.

I know that there are a variety of terminologies for inner world in psychology and other theories including spiritual ones. In this chapter, we will define together a practical definition that is related directly to the process of change.

Deep essence

It's hard to define what deep essence means. It will become clearer during the process that you will go through with this book. In the meantime, we will define your deep essence as the source of your true desire, what you really want from life, which doesn't depend on others.

Feelings

Feelings are the reaction of your deep essence to reality. It includes the emotions that cause physical reactions like crying, laughing, etc.

The inner world is very complicated. Here I'm using thin definitions for it, only to create a basic common understanding. We will expand on deeper essence and feelings in the next chapters.

Thoughts

Thoughts include the words, sentences and images that are running through your mind.

We'll distinguish between thoughts that are essential for your inner communication and unwanted thoughts that are active in the background.

Essential thoughts: thoughts that are related to the present; it's your inner-communication with the external present reality. Essential thoughts are helping you to analyze and decide before taking an action and during it, they are essential to life in the present, and are also the translation of your deep essence to the outside, before you express yourself to the world outside; also on the flipside, your impression of the outside world.

Background (unwanted) thoughts: endless background noise, thoughts that aren't related to the activity in the present. They are all pieces of things from the past, concerns about the future, things that happen in other places. They are unwanted and are usually unstoppable.

To become aware of the background thoughts, perform a simple exercise:

1. Try to relax and clear your mind of all thoughts.
2. Of course, when you're trying to relax, thoughts are arising. Document these thoughts: write every thought down, no matter its meaning, even if it's a strange thought. The thoughts may come faster than you can write, so just write what you can catch. Do it for 2 minutes. It's a lot of writing.

3. When you're done, read your thoughts. As you can see, you intended to think about nothing but thoughts were running through your mind, thoughts that were not related to the present and didn't obey your decision to relax.

Some of these thoughts may be important: concerns, reminders, things not to forget to do, analysis of events that happened in the past, etc. But life is happening in the present, and in order to communicate with reality your thoughts have to be focused only on the present. I know that it's almost impossible to turn off the thoughts but it's necessary for the following process in this book that you focus your mind.

The following chapter will help you to do it, by using the "step-by-step tool to focus your mind."

Chapter 2: Find your focus

The process that's presented to you in this book is guiding you to make a change in your life that begins in your inner world. Therefore, it's important that before doing any reading or practical work, use the following step-by-step tool to focus yourself and minimize the noise of unwanted background thoughts. It's almost impossible to avoid background thoughts completely, but you can minimize their effect.

This process is a practice. In the beginning it can be difficult to practice, but over time it will become easier. Use it before reading a new chapter and doing any practical work from it. You can also use it whenever you want to find your focus.

In this moment, like every moment, probably a lot of endless thoughts run through your mind. Resistance strengthens their existence; therefore the key is to move them to the background. The following tool will help you with that.

Step-by-step tool to find your focus:

Follow these steps by just letting the words lead you. If you prefer with your eyes closed, read the instructions first and then follow them. It's simple and you can memorize them quickly.

1. Sit in a comfortable position, with your spine stretched out.
2. Take 3 deep breaths. On every inhale, feel fresh air filling you; on every exhale feel the air leaving you and taking unwanted things with it.
3. Continue breathing without effort, just breathe.

4. Allow your body to relax and be loose, without expending any effort. Release all the muscles in your body, allow them to be relaxed.

5. Pay attention to your breathing. Focus on the air that leaves your lungs and comes inside.

6. Put your attention on your inner world. Look at the thoughts that are running in your mind now. Look at them from the side, like a witness, observe them running in your mind. Watch them gradually moving away to a cloud. See your thoughts as one cloud. They are moving there, far away. And now, every new thought goes directly to the cloud.

Continue with this exercise for a few minutes. When you feel ready, come back gradually, fully aware now of reality. Stay relaxed.

Chapter 3: Deciding on your top priority change

After reaching the lowest point in my life I discovered one important thing: even when I thought I was at the lowest point, I realized that there is always a lower point. I knew that I had to make a change in life but at that point I didn't know what the change had to be. Life seemed like a whole complex of events carrying on with endless changes, but I didn't know how true that impression actually was.

My journey of life started with developing the ability to make decisions. I realized that I didn't make my own decisions about my life and life was taking me in various directions that were all different from my desires.

It's easy to understand that life is dynamic, always in a state of change and it seems that change is one mixed up complex but if you divide your life into areas, it will be easy to change each area. Therefore we can't change life in general, but have to start in a specific area of life. In fact, it's common knowledge that every completed project has been built in a process, each moment with another piece ("Rome wasn't built in a day"). Changing life is the same, changing one part at a time– one area of life at a time.
According to this attitude you can decide about the area of life that you want to implement a change in and then initiate a process to change it. This Guide will help you to do just that: decide on a goal and fulfill it in your life by yourself.

In setting goals in life, you determine the essence of the change that will be happening and this decision will take you from the present to the desired goal. Between the two points, the present and the goal, there's the journey: your life. Starting to live a life that you control begins with making decisions about goals.

Every decision to set a goal is the beginning of a new journey. The first step is to decide on the area of life that has to be changed now. It means asking yourself, what is the change that's needed in order to fulfill your desire? Maybe you need to make more than one change. But one must be the top priority change. You decide each time on just one change; you can implement multiple changes parallel in your life but decide each time on just one.

The **tool for deciding on the top priority area of life to change** will help you to make the decision. In using the tool, you can decide on the area of life that you want to change in the present as the first step in the process of fulfilling a goal in a specific area of life, and then you can do the same in other areas of life- each time, one process.

Step-by-step for deciding on the top priority area of life to change:

Step 1:
In your notebook, draw a circle that fills the whole page. Write your name in the center.

Step 2:
Around your name, inside the circle, write the areas of life that concern you these days: relationships, health, property (car, house, etc.), money, career, personality, family, well-being, leisure activities, habits, etc.
Location of each area of life around the center of the circle is determined by how much it worries you now. Those that are of more influence and greater importance at present should be closer to the center of the circle, closer to your name.

Step 3:
Look at your circle for a few minutes, look at each area of life and let feelings come up during the process.

Step 4:
For each area of life that appears in the circle, decide the level of your motivation to change it, from 0 to 10. 0 means no desire to change at all and 10 means a strong desire to change. Write the number right next to each area.
Once you're done, you'll have a circle with areas of life and the level of your motivation to change them.

Step 5:
Admire with pride and pleasure what you have created: a map of the areas of your life!

Step 6:
According to the map you can easily decide on what area you want to change. Write the area decided upon in your notebook.
The area of life that I want to change is_____
In this stage, you only use the area of life. During the process that will be presented to you in the next chapters you will focus that area of life and change it according to your vision.

Chapter 4: Acceptance

I remember that when I didn't succeed to create my desired reality I developed a deep resistance to my actual reality. I was flooded with feelings of frustration and anger. It became worse every time I felt disappointed from undesired outcomes in reality. It was mud that I sank deeper into the more I tried to resist it. The light at the end of the tunnel came to me when I discovered acceptance.

Acceptance of existence is the first step in any change.

From resistance to acceptance

When you have desire for a change in life, the same as you are having right now, it means that you probably feel resistance to the undesired thing that you want to change (part of your current reality). To change the undesired you have to first accept it.

It seems like the opposite thing to do --to accept the undesired situation that you want to change-- but that's the idea. If you resist the undesired, you empower it. You have to accept it and in that way, it can be released from your life, and make room for the desire.

The essence of acceptance

When you accept everything in your life, you have the freedom to change everything, including the parts that are undesirable to you because you no longer invest unnecessary energy in something you don't need. You stop holding it, and then you can release it from your life. You understand that there was a reason for the existence of the undesired reality, and you can change it by re-deciding on it.

Part of the purpose of blessings in prayers is acceptance of reality. It's a way to accept a situation even if it's undesired.

The how-to

Acceptance is a way of thinking, an attitude of 'let it be', to accept the undesired situation as much as the desired situation. You believe it has to be, sometimes you don't know the reason for the situation, but you trust that there is a reason for it. Acceptance consists of your opinions and beliefs on the events that are happening in your life, and like the nature of opinion, you can change it. Changing it can stop resistance of the undesired and help to focus on the desire that you want to create.

The next chapter will guide you to accept your undesired existence.

Chapter 5:
Realize and Accept the undesired in the chosen area of life

In my life before, before the journey, I was on one path that was based on the conventional ideals of life: study in university, find a well-paid job, get married, buy a house, have children, pay taxes and be a good person. It all worked for me until the crisis that split my life into two parts: before and after. Before, I had a routine, and a comfortable and secure life; after, a stormy and uncertain life.

After deeper insight into my life, I felt blessed by the crisis: it was the shocking event that I needed in order to implement the change that I actually wanted. But I had wanted to find the way to initiate such changes by myself instead of having the crisis do it for me. My conclusion was that the crisis occurred because I ignored my deep essence. Also, I didn't pay attention to the fact that my life had changed and I hadn't responded to those changes in time.

Getting to a crisis means the change had to be taken sooner. Ignoring change and avoiding making decisions creates a gap that becomes wider until a crisis occurs.

You decided in the last chapter about a top priority change. This change is in the chosen area of life that you need to update, due to the gap that was created between your desires and the reality in the given area of life.

This chapter will guide you to initiate change in your life by understanding your desires and accepting the undesired before the change.

Example: you decide on career as the area of life to change. This means that since you chose your current job there have been changes- you were different than you are today. The reality has also changed since then. In the process of changing, a gap was created between your desires and the reality of your career (new boss, new project, boring routine, etc.). Your desires changed according to your evolvement; you have different expectations for your career. Because of the gap between your desire and the reality, you have to update this area of life and make a decision about a change.

The following process (in this chapter and in the following) will lead you to understand the gap between your desire and the undesired in reality in the chosen area of life that needs to change. According to that understanding, you can realize your desire to change the chosen area, and then accept it as is, which is the step before the change.

Realizing and accepting the undesired

1. Realizing what's undesired about the area of your life.
Think about the area of life that you chose to change and list all the things that concern you and have to change.

2. Accept the undesired about the area of your life.
When you finish, look at the list that you just created. Read the content, it's the present reality that has to change. Observe it like a witness, looking in from the outside. Accept this reality as meant-to-be; without any judgment or criticism or opposition.

Example 1

Area of life that has to be changed: **career.**
Things that concern me:
Low salary
Lack of free time
Emptiness
I find myself getting bored frequently.
I get tired from driving every day in traffic.

Example 2

Area of life than has to be changed: **relationship** (finding the one).
Things that concern me:
Feeling lonely.
Desire to be a family.
Want a partner for inspiration.
Want to be in love.
Someone who sees me as I am without desire to change me.
Feel the excitement of being in a relationship.
Miss intimacy.
Need partner for life.
Want someone close to share the special moments with.

Feel that someone is caring for me.

Example 3

Area of life than has to be changed: **Money.**
Money is not a goal in and of itself but a means to achieve something else. If money concerns you, think about the things that are missing in your life because of money. It could be a new house, saving for college for your children, daily expenses, a trip to an exotic destination, a special hobby, buying a sports car, buying a motorcycle, etc.
Things that concern me:
Lack of money for my daily expenses.

When you are ready, continue with the next chapter.

Chapter 6:
Discover your vision

I came to understand the importance of vision when I met my despair while facing endless barriers on my path to fulfilling my plans. I felt that I had my plans and reality had others. The joke, "You want to make God laugh? Make plans" became my sad story. Every time that I bumped into a barrier it was difficult for me to find the balance between being adaptable to reality and being loyal to my desires.

My process of understanding about coping with barriers led me to discover the essence of vision. It was a door opening on a world that I hadn't known until then.

What is vision?

Vision is the reflection of your desire in reality.

Most of the time, you aren't aware of your vision, but it is the inner guide in your decisions. Every time you make a decision you have the opportunity to express your vision.

Reality is unexpected- sometimes the outcome differs from your plans. To compete with this fact, stay aware of your vision. This will help you to make your decisions while being in the unexpectedness of reality and still stick to your desires.

Example: you decide on a goal, a career change. You feel fatigued at your current job. You want to find an interesting job and at the same time, you want to make a better living. You send your resume to potential companies, do interviews, but despite your best efforts you don't find the position you long for. If this was a real situation, what should you do? Compromise with your desire or continue with the same attempts?

In this example, vision can help by being the link between reality and your desires.

Most of the time, 'vision' is used to describe some transcendental ideals that come from humanity or culture but ideals can also come from your deep essence.

What does deep essence mean?

Your deep essence is your natural state of being. It is freedom to make decisions, your absolute truth, pure you, the source of your desire. It's impossible to define or understand the deep essence as it is because it is abstract, endless, and undefined. It's like trying to define love, an infinite number of words still can't cover the whole of it. It's also like trying to define silence- it's only possible to define it in relative terms, meaning silence can only be measured according to noise.

We can use the terms 'noise' and 'silence' to understand deep essence.

The silence is the deep essence ("you") and the noise is everything else in life that pulls you in other directions ("other").

Your deep essence has no fears, criticism, judgment, obligations, blocks, filters or resistances. It's pure, without ideas that come from the outside world. Even the highest of values, like morals or ideals - -as long as they're not adopted as your truth-- are exterior to your deep essence.

According to this terminology, we can define deep essence as pure you, without the influence of **'other'**.

In every decision there is a range between "you" and "other". When your decision is coming more from "you", it will be according more to your deep essence, and if it's from "other," it will be according more to all that is exterior to you.

In this chapter, we will focus on "you" by exploring your deep essence according to the challenges in reality. In the chapter, "use fears to motivate and to navigate" we will focus on "other" by exploring your fears.

Vision is the reacting of your deep essence to reality. On the one hand, you have your desires and on the other, you have reality. Most of the time, there is a gap between them and this is the essence of life evolvement. That's the reason we set goals in life.

Example one: you have a well-paid job but you decide to make a change. You have a dream to make your hobby into a career and become an artist. You set it as a career goal.

Example two: you have a well-paid job but you decide to make a change- to get a promotion in the company that you work for. You set it as a career goal.

In example one, the gap between your desires and reality is larger compared to example two. That's why your desires in example one will demand more effort and will lead you to a deeper evolvement than those desires in example two.

Vision is the key to initiate the change that will reflect your desires in your present reality.

To explore your vision of the area of life that you want to change, we first have to explore the part of your deep essence that's related to it.

The following process will help you to discover your vision of the area of life you want to change.

Discover your vision

Prepare a 3 column table with these titles:
1. Things that concern you in the present.
2. The best idea to solve your concern.
3. Inner changes.

Use this table for the following process:

Step 1: In the first column, copy the list that you wrote while working in the last chapter- the list with all the things that concern you and you want to change in the chosen area.

Step 2: In the second column, for each item in first column, answer this question:

What is your best idea to change each concern in the first column? In your answer, ignore restraints but stay realistic. The idea must be as efficient as possible and cover the concern but still be able to be implemented in reality.

It's like your best friend tells you about a problem they have. You invest your efforts and think of the best idea that you have to help the friend that you love.

Step 3:   In the third column, write for each item in the second column the change you want to achieve within yourself: a shift in attitude or state of mind, skills, new experiences, etc.

In order to accomplish these changes, ask yourself this question for each item in the second column: if you achieve this, how would that make you feel, what would your state of mind be, or how would your personality be different?

Example 1:

Area of life that has to be changed: **career.**

Things that concern you in the present:	The best idea to solve your concern:	Inner Changes
Lack of free time	Job with less hours	free
Emptiness	Find what makes me feel fulfilled	fulfilled
I find myself getting bored frequently	Challenging job that will be dynamic	interested
I get tired from driving in traffic every day	Somewhere closer or consider working from home.	comfortable
Low salary	Well-paid job- I'm worth it	satisfied

Example 2:

Area of life than has to be changed: **relationship** (finding the one).

Things that concern you in the present:	The best idea to solve your concern	Inner Changes
Feeling lonely	To be with someone that makes me feel not alone	Companionship, feeling accompanied
Desire to have a family	Relationship with a person that wants family	Growing up, responsibility
Want a partner that inspires me	Feel inspired when I meet him/her	Inspired
Want to be in love	To be in love when I'm with him/her	Harmony and love
Person who sees me as I am without desire to change me	Someone that loves me as I am	Love my self
Feel the excitement of being in a relationship	Feel the excitement when I'm with him/her	Alive
Miss intimacy	Feel comfortable to open up and be intimate with him/her	Intimacy
Need a partner for life	Want to be with him/her more and more	Real friendship
Want someone close to share the special moments with	Every moment with her/him becomes special to me	Romantic
Feel that someone is caring for me	She/he is there for me whenever I need them	Secured

Example 3
Area of life than has to be changed: **money.**

If you decide about money as a goal, in this stage, it's better to discuss the goal that would supply you more money. I can presume this goal is career change (if you have other possibilities, use them). In this example, we change the goal, from money to career, and money is the major concern (of course you can add more concerns, if you have any, in your present career).

Area of life that concerns you that has to be changed: **career.**

Things that concern you in the present:	The best idea to solve your concern	Inner Changes
Lack of money	Finding a better-paid job	Confidence and balance

This table will serve as a vision about your goal. It reflects your desire, the practical thing to do about it, and the change that will take place in your inner world or self. It means that the content in the second column is your reaction to the present reality that will ensure you fulfill your desires, and will make you feel the things detailed in the third column.

The table will be a guiding light for the following process that will be in the next chapters of this Guide. The second column is your vision- it contains the best idea to change your concerns in your present reality. You will specify the vision with actions in the next chapters. The third column is the outcome of what you achieve in the second column. It contains the changes that will take place in your inner world—and in fact, these changes are the reason for this entire process. We will also enter into more detail with this in the next chapters.

Read the table again and ask yourself if it covers your whole vision. According to your answer, decide if you want to add more to the table or not.

When you are ready, continue with the next chapter.

Chapter 7:
Making your own decisions

In my life, making decisions was always a big issue for me. I found myself trying to avoid doing so whenever I could. But life has its own rhythm and every time I didn't make a decision, life did for me. Only after I started being in a state of awareness towards my life did I realize that I was in undesired places in my life because of the fact that I wasn't making my own decisions.

Making decisions was one of the main areas on my journey of life. I explored the way to make decisions efficiently.   From this experience I gained knowledge about decision-making and also developed a self-training tool for making decisions.

Let's begin with some knowledge that will shed light on the process of making decisions to understand what the right decision is and why it is difficult to make it.

Points of knowledge to shed light on the decision-making process:

1. Being in dilemma.

There are simple decisions that are easy to make: the options are clear, the right option is right in front of you and the other possibilities are small and in the shadows, so it's easy to decide. But there are decisions that aren't black and white. The reason for this is that every option has advantages and disadvantages.

Example: you are in the moment before making a decision about buying a new house. There are two houses you've been considering, both fit your requirements but differ in one way. One house is far from your work but with a great view and close to the park. The other is close to your work but in a busy area of the city, with no view, and is far from parks. You have a dilemma: the advantages of the park versus the advantages of living close to work. So, if this was actually you, which house would you prefer?

2. Decision creates the certain in the uncertain.

During the moments after you understand you need a change but before you make a decision about what the change will be, you are in a state of uncertainty. The decision makes the uncertain, certain.

Going back to the last example about buying a house, during the search you are in uncertainty with your life regarding the place where you'll live. You don't know where that place will be. After making the decision about which house to buy, you are in a state of certainty about your living situation for the foreseeable future.

3. Every decision has risks and potential value.

For every decision, there is the potential to get what you want and there is a risk of getting an undesired outcome. In most of cases, the level of risk influences the duration of time it takes to makes the decision.

If the decision leads you to the expected result, you get the value that you desire. But if not, you don't get it, and it's possible to also lose something (money, etc.) and have negative feelings (disappointment, frustration, etc).

Example one: you are in a moment before making a decision about which romantic restaurant to take your significant other. It's extremely important to you because it's for celebrating their birthday.

Example two: you want to decide on a restaurant for lunch during your work day.

It's clear that in example one the risk that results from your decision is higher compared to example two and therefore it's probable that in example one the decision will take longer to make compared to example two.

Let's get deep inside the issue of making decisions. In order to do that, let's understand the process.

The three stages of making decisions:

1. Gathering information.
To understand your choices you need to understand your desires first. When you want ice-cream, before buying it you just have to look at the flavors and then choose. Therefore, the stage of gathering information is only screening the flavors by look or taste. Before buying a car, you check the features that meet your needs and decide. Therefore, the stage of gathering information is to understand the features of different cars that are in your budget (by meeting a salesman or reading about them or talking with friends, etc.).

2. Weighing options.
It's the moment when you have in your mind all the options that you gathered, not necessarily all the possibilities that exist, but only those that attracted you or succeeded to grasp you when you were gathering information. You screen these options and weigh them.

3. Cutting of and continuing life with one choice.
This is the stage of deciding on one of the options that makes a change in your life. It can be a small change like eating mint ice-cream or a much bigger one, like with whom you want to spend your life with. Both are decisions.
Now that we have a slightly better understanding of making decisions, let's focus the issue and go deeper, in order to neutralize causes that disturb you when making decisions.

Big decisions and small decisions can take the same amount of time:
After gathering the information about the possibilities, you then weigh them as your options until cutting of and deciding on one of them. Sometimes, there are decisions that become dilemmas- it's hard to choose, and the decision is postponed because of this. It's easy to delay such decisions because they're big ones.
Our mind is so powerful that it can do huge amounts of analysis in less than a second. For making big decisions, like buying a house, you have to consider dozens of factors (location, size, floor, etc). To make a decision about reservations in restaurants you have to consider a few factors. Neurology research shows that our mind can do billions of operations in less than a second. So, in that case, both decisions can be made in less than a second and the gap between the two decisions is a split second.

Therefore, big decisions only require the gathering of more information when compared to small decisions. It's only a technical issue: gathering enough information and making the decision as you do with small decisions. So, no need to postpone such decisions.

The unnecessary delay in decision-making opens a door to doubts and fears
The time between the desire to change until the decision is made, is the grey area of life that raises doubts in you about your decision to change, and it also raises fears about the future. It's unnecessary to stay in this stage for long.

Therefore,
it is better to make a decision and assume a certain amount of risk rather than delaying the decision out of fear of that risk. Every

moment is a new page and you can make another decision if you want to change the outcome after the initial decision.

But,

as with everything in life, it has to be in balance. It's important to make the decision but at the same time, it must be the right decision- not just one made in haste in order to have it made and done with.

The right decision

The right decision is not "right or wrong" but is determined by how much it is in tune with your needs. What is the right decision? We are working toward understanding it throughout the entire book. The answer will become clear during the process that you are undertaking.

Tool for self-training to make decisions

The next day train yourself in making daily decisions. There are decisions that you are making almost every moment of the day, some of them so fast that they are almost automatic: clothes to wear to the office, faster route to drive in rush hour, what to eat at lunch, accepting an invitation of your colleague to get a beer after work, to do an assignment that you forgot to do in the office or delaying it for tomorrow, etc.

In this stage you will focus on daily decisions to shed light on the process of making decisions and discover if you have any points of difficulty.

Follow these instructions for tomorrow (read it now and implement tomorrow):

First, set 3 alarms, spread throughout the day. When an alarm goes off, stop in your daily routine and take a moment to fill in the following table.

Focus on the last decision that you made. It can be any decision, even a small one. Fill in the following table.

1st column: the decision.

2nd Column: In the moment of making the decision, what was the risk, the consequences if things went wrong?

3rd Column: In the moment of making the decision, what was the value if the decision were successful?

4th Column: Was it a quickly-made decision or were you dawdling or even postponing it? This question is related to the last 2 stages of the decision-making process: weighing possibilities and then cutting off with one option.

You will have finished when you have filled in this table, three rows about three decisions that you made during the day.

Look at the table, and focus on the decisions that weren't fast or you had difficulty in making. What was the reason for the difficulty?

Fears because of the risks? Not sure about the value? Something else?

Observe the risk and the value, and think about the difficulties in getting to the decision, was the difficulty was justified?

Continue with this awareness when making your decisions during next few days.

Example:

The decision	Risk (in the moment of decision-making)	Value (in the moment of decision-making)	Was it quickly made?
Accept the invitation for a high school reunion?	Feeling embarrassed by the entire situation	Enjoy seeing friends from the past	No
Choose place to eat lunch	Food may not be tasty	Enjoy a good meal	Yes
Choose clothes for my best friend's wedding	Not looking my best and properly honoring the occasion	Honoring this important day in my friend's life	No

When you are ready, continue with the next chapter.

Chapter 8:
Decide on the goal

At this point, you have decided on the area in your life that you want to change, and also discovered your vision of it. Now it's time to decide on the goal, which means to choose the destination point that you want to reach.

You probably have a rough idea of what the goal is, but it may be vague or blurry. To take it from your mind and bring it into reality, you have to translate the idea into a practical form: which means to make the goal a reachable target.

In order to be realistic, you must have a certain amount of faith that you can reach it in the near future, even just a little faith is sufficient.

Examples to illustrate the range of faith: to earn a million dollars in two years is a low probability goal for an unemployed person, but realistic, so it's worthwhile to have a certain amount of faith in it; meeting one's significant other in a year is a high probability goal for a single person in their thirties, so hopefully they're able to have a high amount of faith in it; to live on Mars is impossible, so it's an unrealistic goal, so it would be counterproductive to have faith in it.

Regarding the particular area of life that you want to change, what is your goal?

Write on a new page in your notebook:

My goal is _____ (fill in the blank).

Congratulations! You set a new goal in your life.

1. Self-commitment to your decision.

A goal is a commitment to a new way of life that you've decided on. In order to achieve the goal you have to continue forward until you achieve it. Although there might be barriers, you continue to keep your vision alive.

Commit to yourself in any way: by writing, thinking, shouting it- please use at least one way to express your promising to yourself that you will continue forward until reaching the goal.

You can use the words 'I commit to myself to continue until I reach the goal '_____' (write your goal here).

A few words about commitment: it has negative associations, a sense of debt to others. In this process, it's a promise only to yourself to continue through the upcoming obstacles until you make it.

2. Make the announcement to the world.

A decision about a goal is a declaration to the world about fulfilling your desire. It's like a king that announces to his circle of attendants his desire; he knows the power of that expression, words that become reality.

Pick at least one person to tell of your decision. Announce it as a plan with complete confidence of its coming true.

3. Celebration.

Celebrate your decision to fulfill the goal. It's a big reason for celebration. Celebrate it knowing that it will happen (please do not be afraid of disappointment or of any superstition, believe in yourself). Find the way to celebrate by doing something that you like and/or buy yourself a small gift. You deserve it. I usually celebrate such occasions by buying myself Swiss chocolate and walking on the beach. Of course, I don't need any reason for chocolate or walking on the beach but every time that there is reason for doing that, I use it.

When you are ready, continue with the next chapter.

Chapter 9:
Use fears to motivate and to navigate

As I was progressing with my journey I met my fears quite often, without being aware of their influence: virtual walls that were limiting my evolvement. During my attempts to cope with the barriers in my life, I found myself grappling with my fears; they blocked me every time I tried to initiate a change in my life. My first reaction while coping with my fears was to resist them, and I also tried to break them like walls. After getting tired from 'fighting windmills', I stopped my attempts. I came to understand that resistance to fears doesn't work, and that's why I searched for ways to live with the fears. When I lived at peace with my fears, I was surprised how easy life became. By living with the fears and even using them as a partner, evolvement in life becomes possible.

In this stage of the process, you attempt to implement your change in life and therefore fear arises. Even without being aware of it, its influence is in the background: shading the excitement as well as weakening your motivation to move forward. Fears arise every time that you challenge yourself, in which case you initiate change in your life. Although they have a bad reputation, fears are essential for your life's evolvement.

In this step you can learn with a simple self-implementation method how to recognize the fears and use them as an engine that can not only empower your efforts towards the goal but can also help you with all challenges in life. The way to do it is to harness your fears according to your desires, in this case your goal.

In order to harness your fears according to your goal, let's understand first what fear's purpose and essence is in our lives:

1. Warning sign.

To warn you before something might happen before you take an action in an uncertain world. You can look at it as a road sign that warns you before a sharp bend in the road, or an alarm in the navigation system- you respond with action, like reducing the speed of the car or driving more carefully. It means that you become more aware of the continued road and take actions in time.

In the case of the planning and taking actions along the way to the goal, fear is helping you to stay focused on your actions in order to achieve the planned goal, and to prepare yourself to be ready for upcoming changes by planning the correct actions and adapting your patterns and habits to the changes that you plan.

2. Excitement.

There is a relationship between fear and excitement. When fears appear, feelings of excitement also arise. The essence of this relationship is that fear is functioning as a trigger that creates feelings of excitement: whenever feelings of fear appear, there are feelings of excitement also.

3. Resistance to fear empowers it.

Fear has a negative connotation because of trying to resist it instead of working with it. Resistance to fear can create negative consequences, such as anxiety. It is these negative consequences that cause you to resist fear, but it is not fear itself. It is a loop of resistance and negative consequence that you can break free of. Therefore, it's better to benefit from fear and not to resist it.

In this chapter, you will work with fears and use them to empower your motivation and navigate through the challenges you will face.

You can do this by using the tool 'use fears to empower your motivation and navigate through the challenges'.

The tool uses fears to empower your motivation and navigate through the challenges:

Follow these instructions (you can also read them and then follow them with closed eyes):

1. Think and feel about the moment that you reach your goal:

a. Imagine the process that you have gone through until you reach this point. It does not have to be a precise future plan, just scenes of it, like a movie that runs in fast forward, until the destination.

b. Allow feelings and thoughts to arise. They're probably mixed up, let them be as they are.

c. Ask yourself this question: what are you afraid could happen along the path before reaching the destination? Try to get as many answers as you can.

Do that only for a few minutes- don't get too deep into your fears.

Take a deep breath and continue to the next step.

2. In your notebook make a table with 4 columns, with the following titles: Fears and Worries, Possible Consequences, Actions I will take, and the way I will feel.

First column: write the things that you are afraid of or worry about regarding the fulfillment of the goal. Detail everything: write all the fears and worries that arise, don't resist or judge them, just write them.

Second column: look at the fears and worries in the first column. For each fear or worry, answer this question: what is the consequence that every fear points towards?

Third column: what would be your actions to avoid the possible consequences that might happen as described in the second column?

Fourth column: what would you feel after having succeeded with your actions?

Example 1: career change- online marketing.

Fears and Worries	Possible Consequences	Actions I will take	The way I'll feel
Afraid of failing	1. Lose money 2. Feel like a failure 3. Feel low confidence	Prepare business plan with the assistance of a professional consultant	1. Secure with the knowledge that I can make money on my own 2. Satisfaction 3. Feel high confidence with myself
Worry about difficulties	Can't continue moving forward	Focus my efforts and give what I have in order to succeed	Strong with the feeling that I can do anything
Afraid to make changes in my career	Changes can cause bad things to happen	Focus on my new business and the advantages of implementing it	Satisfaction and enjoyment from my career

Example 2: finding my significant other

Fears and Worries	Possible Consequences	Actions I will take	The way I'll feel
Getting hurt again	My heart would break again	Surround myself with loving people	I'll be ready for any eventuality
I'll never find 'the one'	Staying along forever	Promise myself to continue trying	Full of hope for the future
I'll end up sacrificing my needs in the future relationship	Losing myself	Find the one that will take me as I am without any desire to change me	Unity and love

Look at your table with pride. It was a deep process of understanding and focusing.

Use the second column of the table (Possible consequences) as focal points of your attention - things that you have to be focused on during your actions until reaching your desired goal.

During your journey towards the goal, allow the feelings and the inner changes to take place. With this table you open a window to the future in order to peek at your future feelings and changes: you can see them now in the 4th column (The way I'll feel). It can help you to prepare yourself now for eventualities in the future. When you can see or visualize something before it happens, it will be easier for you to accept your fears as you travel along your path.

This process is the beginning of your awareness of the fears in your life. You can keep the table open for more fears that may appear in the near future. Write them down and work with them according to the instructions.

When you are ready, continue with the next chapter.

Chapter 10:
Making an inspired environment

My journey has been accompanied by a lot of changes in my attitude about life. In a short period, I developed a different perspective about the essence of life. The changes were so sharp that I found myself becoming more distant from others, even from my family. I was dividing the world into two groups: those that were practicing the way of awareness (the spiritual world) and those that were not (the material world). Objectively speaking, my life was unbalanced and it didn't last for long- the radicalization of the spiritual attitude in my life bumped into barriers that real life was setting. I realized that I had to gather myself and find the balance in life between the two worlds, integrate them together into my surrounding reality, by creating an inspired and balanced environment.

In this step, you're invited to make your inspired environment:
1. Adjust your day-to-day life for the upcoming change by preparing an inspiring and encouraging environment that welcomes the change.
2. Include in your daily routine reminders of your goal.
3. Expand your creativity by setting up an attractive and stimulating environment.

The following process will guide you to create an inspiring environment, not only for the benefit of fulfilling a specific goal, but also for life in general.
1. **Close circle of people**: make sure that you have a circle of people that are close to you that will understand you and the changes that you implement, people you can talk with openly

without concerns or obligations. It's people that you have frequent interaction with and that understand you and listen to what you have to say. You feel comfortable with them, they encourage you whenever you need it and inspire you; you feel that they are partners in life.

It could be from your family, from work, your significant other, etc. Think about it, do you have this circle of people in your life?

2. **Physical place and time for yourself:** make sure that you have a place for yourself before or after obligations (work, errands, chores, etc). It's a place where you feel comfortable and quiet, to be with yourself: a place on the beach or a place in the park or a quiet coffee shop that you can visit on your way home. It's a time when you can feel free from obligations, feel freedom to be quiet and peaceful within yourself, just to be. Even if just for a few minutes every day.

3. **Information:** we are living in a world where information is an essential player in every process. Today information is highly accessible, with minimum effort. You can use the high accessibility of information in order to make your process richer by expanding your knowledge of it.

The following instructions will help you to create your inspiring environment based on these elements: close circle of people, physical place, time for yourself, and information:
1. List the people that you feel comfortable talking with about personal issues, and sharing your goal with.

When you're done, look at the list. Mention to each one every so often the progress you're making towards your goal. It's important that they're on the same page as you with regards to the change you desire and are working towards.

2. Use the internet to create a daily environment of virtual world information: subscribe to newsletters, magazines, blogs and webinars to get frequent content about subjects that are related to your goal. Create in yourself the habit of reading from them every day.

3. Create a virtual informal support community for yourself: join social networks, forums, virtual communities: express yourself there, support others, be supported by others, and learn from the experience of others. Here you can interact with people that have similar goals to your own.

4. Create an inspiration board for the goal and for future goals. You can use online applications for this, but I prefer the old-school way with cork board- tangible materials that emphasize your goal more. For every goal, use a picture on the board that will make you feel inspired by the goal. It's easy and comfortable to hang up pictures. You can cut pictures from magazines or print them. For example, an image of a man riding a bicycle in nature for inspiration towards the goal of losing weight.

When you are ready, continue with the next chapter.

Chapter 11:
To be the Creator of your life

One of the major purposes of my journey was to take control of my life: making decisions and making them happen without dependence on external factors in life, including other people. I succeeded with the taking control and things started to get in line but at the same time I lost the essence of life. I discovered that losing a certain amount of control to accept the uncertain is necessary to maintain a level of excitement, fun, and evolvement in life. I immediately corrected the path of my journey; I went from taking control to becoming the Creator of my life. This means finding the balance between taking control of life and living peacefully with the uncertain.

Taking control of life

In order to find the way to live a fulfilling life, where I could live my life according to my choices, I came to understand that the uncertain in life arises as a major factor in the equation. As a researcher, I couldn't use it as a factor, I needed to discover the missing factor, a means to explain the uncertainty in life. But at the same time, I understood that there is no logical explanation about this area of life and there are only religious explanations and abstract, mystical explanations (luck, destiny, coincidence, etc.) that regard these issues as they are without question.

That's why, with the assumption that I'm the only one responsible for all the events happening in my life, including the unexpected, I was researching to find the conditions that had to be incorporated into my attitude in order to cause the magic to happen: to make plans and have them happen.

Letting go by accepting the uncertainty in life

The uncertain sets challenges in daily life. It means making decisions and acting in the present without guarantee about the outcome in the future. It seems opposite of the basic desire to control life but uncertainty is an essential factor in life. It creates the excitement from experiencing new things, evolvement by fulfilling all potential, empowering personality with challenges, motivating so that one continues initiating actions. Living without uncertainty is to live life without surprises; there is nothing to look forward to and there is no excitement about the future.

Finding control of life in the uncertain

The uncertain and taking control seem like factors that pull in opposite directions, but like all seeming contradictions in life, the balance of these opposite essences creates the delicate texture of a full life.

For example, you make a decision to have a new business: writing and selling books on Amazon. The process is having a vision, an idea to write about, then writing it, designing the cover, submitting it to Amazon, and finally actively promoting it and hoping for the best. In this example, you're taking control when making a decision, setting it as a goal, and the following actions. But the goal depends on uncertain factors such as the amount of buyers of the book. In the moment when you're writing your book, you don't know what the outcome of publishing it will be. The uncertainty of the future motivates you to put in your maximum efforts in the present in order to achieve the desired goal in the future. At the present you don't know what the exact actions to succeed are but you can know that if you do your best you have a high probability of succeeding, and in case of failure you understand that you have to change something, you change it and try again and again until you succeed. In this way you realize your potential and are in evolvement.

The next two chapters will guide you to find the balance between taking control and living with uncertainty by believing in yourself and doing your best without a guarantee of the outcome ('empowering your self-belief'). You will find the magic of summoning your desires in the uncertain reality ('find the magic in your life'). These are the two keys for you to become the creator of your life.

Chapter 12:
Empowering your self-belief

When you have plans for the future, in this case goals, it means there is a certain amount of probability that they will take place but there is no guarantee- there are other factors that affect the probability.

Examples: you decide to do a sports activity one hour a day. It's a goal that depends on your efforts. If you set this goal in your schedule and commit to this activity, it will happen. Plans like having a child, finding a significant other, success in business, or recovery from chronic disease, depend not only on your effort, but also on other factors. This means that if a person plans any of them now in the present there isn't a guarantee that they will happen for certain in the future. There is a common opinion about life that we live in an uncertain world and according to it, we make plans, try our best, then maybe they will happen and maybe not.
There is a bridge between trying to take control and living in an uncertain world and this bridge is self-belief. You'll be surprised at the power of self-belief in your life.

The following chapter will help you understand the power of self-belief, and also help you to implement it in your life. You probably already have a sense of what self-belief is as a whole, but in order to discover and understand this whole picture, we need to first divide it into small pieces and explore them. Then you will be able to implement this whole picture of self-belief in your life and benefit from the power of it.

What is belief?

Belief is made up of a bundle of statements, world views, and assumptions that characterize a person's behavior, decisions, and thoughts on life events-most of the time without any awareness of them.

Self-belief is your belief about yourself while you interact in the world.

Explanations and rules about the connection between experiences, beliefs and life events:

1. The past influences the future.

From your point of view in the present, beliefs are created in the past and have an influence on the future.

The creation of beliefs is made up of life events from the past. Every event, according to the way you experience it, leaves its impression: feelings, conclusions, statements, opinions. They are the material that beliefs are created from.

Present beliefs influence present behavior and decisions about the future. Beliefs have an influence on the future events of your life. Your beliefs influence your behavior, which in turn, influence all future events. If your beliefs coincide with your goal, then they will empower it. Otherwise, your beliefs will always be working against it.

Example: a person that grew up with parents that encouraged him to be independent; they praised him on every decision he made; they avoided criticism when they saw him making decisions they didn't agree with. He felt their unconditional love.

In the present, as an adult, he's being influenced by the past experiences from his childhood. He is an independent person and can easily make decisions, with self-motivation, and his self-belief encourages him in his decisions and his actions. So, when he decides to start his own business, it's a realistic possibility according to his beliefs about his independence. His self-belief empowers his efforts to succeed.

Of course there are other beliefs that may influence decisions about career and also other factors that influence personality. We'll discuss them later. Here, for the example, we used only one factor in order to explain how the past influences the present and future.

2. Belief is made of subjective impressions about objective events.

Because the material of beliefs is subjective experiences and impressions, the same objective event may create a belief within one person that is different within another person.

For example, a father that taught his children to fix broken devices at home, as part of his vision that his boys be independent with their lives. During his teaching he assumed a tough attitude and criticized them every time they failed; he wanted them to be perfect. One of the brothers had a bad impression of the father's method of guidance. It influenced him in all the actions he took- he integrated his father's criticism into himself and he tries to do every action perfectly. He hesitates before doing anything- he is afraid of making mistakes and in the end, he develops a belief that he has a low probability of succeeding. His brother had a different impression. He enjoys obeying and he developed a soldier's discipline. He enjoys completing assignments and he developed a belief that his actions will lead to success. He doesn't hesitate before any of his actions, he just does them.

3. **Beliefs influence the reality of your life in two spheres:** the physical world and the world beyond, sometimes referred to as the 'spiritual' world.

Sphere 1: the physical world- your actions in reality. We can look at it this way: behavior designs your actions in reality, and beliefs are a designer of behavior. Therefore, you influence your reality according to your beliefs.

Example: you decide to do a sports activity for one hour a day.

If you believe in being consistent and self-disciplined and you behave according to your beliefs, you will succeed in implementing the goal in your life. You determine your reality with the actions you take.

Sphere 2: the essence of the world beyond, the probability that an upcoming event will happen, usually called luck, destiny or other traditional explanations. The strength of your belief directly correlates with the probability that the event will happen.

Example: you decide to set having a successful start-up as a goal. You can invest your efforts in doing that, to be consistent and self-disciplined, creative and do as all entrepreneurs do, but you aren't sure you will succeed, you only have a certain probability of success.

The probability of upcoming events is according to your beliefs. If you have a strong belief about yourself with the vision of a start-up, for example, the probability of succeeding will go in the same direction: the more you believe you will succeed with the start-up, the more likely it is to happen in reality. To emphasize this point, there is no room for other explanations like luck, destiny, coincidence or timing. If you believe and you act according to your belief, it will happen.

When trying to analyze the impact of belief on life in terms of the probability of upcoming events, it's hard to accept it according to logical thinking.

This chapter is a theoretical and practical attempt to explain and prove this, but it's hard to catch it in your consciousness, so the best way to achieve this is to first believe in it (believe in the power of belief) and then try it in your life according to the second part of this chapter. It will then become something you come to accept in your logical mind.

4. **Linear correlation between experiences, beliefs and future events**: the power of a belief depends on the level of impression from past events, and reflects the influence on future events. The stronger the impression an event leaves, the stronger the belief created will be, and the more influence it will have on future events.

For example: you win the lottery and this gives you a deep experience with money, from which you formed a strong impression about earning money. Before, you had beliefs about money, but after the deep experience with the lottery, you develop a stronger belief about money: it's easy to earn money. It's a belief that there is a high probability that your efforts will earn you easy money in the future.

The direction of belief (positive/ negative) is created according to the outcome of past experience. Positive impressions from past events will create positive beliefs about it, and the same happens with negative impressions. Whether they're positive or negative is subjective.

Example 1: you book a vacation on a cruise. You enjoy it; you have good experiences during your vacation. You develop a belief that a cruise is an enjoyable way to spend a vacation. So, next time, if you book a cruise again, you believe you will enjoy it.

Example 2: you book a vacation on a cruise. You don't enjoy it; you have bad experiences during the vacation. You develop a belief that a cruise is not an enjoyable way to spend vacation. So, next time, if you book a cruise again, you hope you'll enjoy it, but you have a certain amount of belief that you won't enjoy it.

5. Belief can empower one goal and weaken another.

Example: a child hears his parents argue about money. The argument left a strong impression on him; he developed his world-view and opinions around the argued subjects: money and relationships. The development of beliefs is not strictly caused (if.... then...) by the specific event, but depends on other experiences as well. If he developed a belief that "money is dirty" as an adult, this belief would not align with the goal of being a rich man. It would weaken his efforts to achieve that goal, but could empower another goal: being spiritual.

6. Beliefs are a complicated network of connections.

Beliefs are created and influenced by every day events, which means that during a lifetime there is a lot of activity with beliefs. It's a complicated fabric woven out of those things that make up life: daily events and your reaction to them, which are based on impressions, feelings, experiences, world views, opinions and assumptions formed throughout life.   This is the reason that it is hard to see the influence of beliefs: you can only see it when you look at the whole picture of your life and normally we live in the point of view of our everyday life, which are only small pieces of that whole.

7. Routine creates a fog around the influence of belief.

It's easy to ignore the influence of beliefs. The routine of everyday actions hides the influence of beliefs and shuts off awareness. That's why events can surprise you but that doesn't mean that you didn't create them. It means you weren't aware of the attitude that created them.

8. Every moment is a new page in the book of life.

You have the freedom to renew your beliefs at any moment according to your experiences, no matter what the belief was before, and how long its duration was.

For example, take a person that grew up with hardworking parents. He developed the belief that 'the way to earn a living is by working hard'. As an adult, according to that belief, he worked hard for money. It was a routine for him and he continued with it for years, until he came across a book that left a strong impression on him. Taking the book to heart, he realized that there are easier ways to earn money. He talks about it with other people and he gets reinforcement about it, then gradually changes his belief from 'earning a living is by working hard' to 'earning a living is easy', and decides to make a change in his career.

9. Combinations of beliefs create larger, complex beliefs in different areas of life.

Any combination of beliefs creates major belief. It works like combinations of pixels that create a picture on the screen; as individual units or as a small group of units, there is no picture. Only the accurate combination of pixels creates the picture. This is case with beliefs: accurate combination creates a major belief about an area of life.

10. It's hard to realize how huge the impact of beliefs is on our life.

It's hard to realize that we are creating our life and accept the influence that our beliefs have on our life. I was convinced of the role that beliefs play in my life only after I saw it with my own eyes.

This Guide can provide you the opportunity to do that in the next part of the chapter. You have the chance to change your beliefs and align them with your goal, after which you can 'see the magic happen'.
In other words, realize the power of beliefs on your life.

What can you do to use the knowledge of beliefs in your life?

1. Awareness that leads to being positive.

Change begins with your awareness. This chapter presents you with the knowledge about beliefs in order to empower your awareness of the influence your beliefs have on your life, and encourage you to choose an attitude towards life that will empower your efforts to fulfill your goals. It's an understanding that you are responsible for what's happening in your life, according to a simple rule: the more you choose a positive attitude, the more the events in your life will be positive. It's a simple but powerful truth.

2. Using the do-it-yourself tool for reprograming your self-beliefs.

In my personal life journey, after I was exposed to various sources of knowledge about beliefs, my awareness of beliefs changed. I believed in myself, and maintained a positive attitude in my life. I set goals, initiated actions to fulfill them, and had a strong belief that my desired change would happen. The changes in my life appeared according to my plans. I was convinced of my ability to fulfill my goals, but I had a hard time with stubborn negative events that were still showing up in my life. I understood that something was missing in my knowledge.

I decided to look for a deeper understanding of the influence of self-belief on my life. I wanted to put my knowledge about self-beliefs under a magnifying glass, and test the correlation of my self-belief in the present with the upcoming events in the future. With this measurement, I wanted to understand the level of probability that an event would happen (beyond my actions), according to my belief, with the purpose of replacing explanations of luck, destiny or coincidence.

After a few years of long and complicated research, I exposed to my deep understanding the relationship between self-belief and the probability of an upcoming event. I understood that the knowledge I had about self-belief was true: my awareness and changing attitude are factors that influence my life, but I was still influenced by beliefs that were created in the past. They were still creating my attitude at that moment and that had to be changed in order to create new beliefs. But my attitude couldn't change because of the belief that still fed it. This phenomenon was a strange feedback loop of attitudes and beliefs that was in process of changing. It was a spiral structure that changed but in very slow motion (I promise to go into more detail about the full outcome of the research on another opportunity).

I wanted to implement a deep and faster change that would help me fulfill my goals. For this reason, I developed a self-implementation tool that will be a link between my new attitude and my past attitude, in order to adjust my self-belief to my goals.

This tool is presented for your benefit in the next part of this chapter: Step-by-step tool for reprograming your self-beliefs according to your goal. It will help you to reprogram the beliefs that you have carried up until now and adjust them based on your decision about the goal that you to want to fulfill in the near future.

Step-by-step tool for reprograming your self-beliefs according to your goal:

This tool will take you through a deep process, the deeper you get into your feelings, thoughts and attitudes, the more the process will succeed. It's recommended to work through this process on several different occasions.

Step 1:
Write your goal: My goal is _____ (write your goal here).
Example: My goal is to have my own online marketing business.

Step 2:
Look at the words you wrote in step one, and think and imagine yourself moving along the path from your present point to your goal. You can close your eyes while doing this for a deeper view. Allow any feelings to arise, it could be happiness, disappointment, excitement, fears, frustration, etc.

Step 3:
Write your thoughts that are related to the goal. Use associations with the goal. There is no right or wrong answer: write every thought or opinion that comes up, no matter if it's positive or negative, without analyzing or criticizing or judging, just shoot, like you do in brainstorming. Use these questions as guidelines. You don't have to answer every question. These are just to get your mind working:
- What are your opinions about the goal?
- What do you know about the goal?
- Why do you think the goal may come true?
- What are your weaknesses regarding the goal?
- What are your strengths regarding the goal?
- Why do you think the goal may not come true?

- What are your concerns about the goal?
- Why do you think you deserve to fulfill the goal?
- What would be your challenges in fulfilling the goal?

Examples
I've always wanted to be independent with my job.
It's probably not for me.
I have low chances of achieving it.
I can earn a lot of money.
It's too hard for me.
It's about time to start a business of my own.
I'm not sure I have the skills for it.
I'm not good enough to do it.
I failed last time and probably will again.
I'm jealous of people who succeed in their career.
It's better for others, I'm not sure I have the skills to do it.

When you're done writing the list, it's recommended to take a break and then come back for another round and continue with this list. Do this on several occasions- every time you'll be exploring another layer of your inner world that's related to the goal. It's deep and you need to discover it. The deeper you go into it, the more the process will be life-changing.

Step 4:
Go through the list and mark with an asterisk the statements that you think would weaken your efforts to fulfill the goal or statements that oppose your attempts to achieve the goal.
Example:
I've always wanted to be independent with my job.
*It's probably not for me.
*I have low chances of achieving it.
I can earn a lot of money.
*It's too hard for me.

It's about time to start a business of my own.
*I'm not sure I have the skills for it.
*I'm not good enough to do it.
*I failed last time and probably will again.
*I'm jealous of people who succeed in their career.
*It's better for others, I'm not sure I have the skills to do it.

Step 5:
Rephrase every marked sentence, so they will be positive reinforcement for your fulfilling the goal. It means deleting the negative words or changing the meaning, in order to create a statement that is in line with achieving the goal.

Example:
I've always wanted to be independent with my job.
It's probably ~~not~~ for me.
I have ~~low~~ high chances of achieving it.
I can earn a lot of money.
It's not too hard for me.
It's about time to start a business of my own.
I'm ~~not~~ sure I have the skills for it.
I'm ~~not~~ good enough to do it.
I failed last time and probably ~~it will happen again~~ this time things will go differently and I will succeed.
I'm ~~jealous~~ full of inspiration from people that succeed with their career.
It's ~~better~~ good for others, and good for me, I ~~not~~ sure I have the skills to do it.

Step 6:
Look at the list for several minutes, without purpose, just stare at the sentences and the words that are creating them.

Step 7:

Cut (or copy to a clean page) the page with the list from your notebook and put it in a visible place where you can look at it every day, like at your desk, and for week, read it every time that you see it, even if that is every 5 minutes; treat it like a mantra. Return to this process every time that you meet with doubts about your efforts on your path to fulfilling the goal.

When you are ready, continue with the next chapter.

Chapter 13:
Find the magic in your life

My path in life was illuminated when I found the option to create my reality according to my goals. It was the sunbeam that I had been waiting for, that opened me up to another world: a world of magic. I explored the hidden force that makes reality happen- that puts all of the events of reality into their proper place, like pieces of a puzzle. Suddenly life made sense to me: I had an explanation for the unexplained in life. As a logical person with a scientific attitude, I used analysis tools to understand the mechanism behind it and I also wanted to discover the way to make it practical. The outcome is presented for you in this chapter: a guided tool for creating your reality.

What is the meaning of creating reality?

Before we dive into the essence of creating reality, let's understand what creating reality actually means.

You can influence your reality with physical actions that express your desire. You take an action in reality, and it replies with the happening of events.

For example, you have a desire to meet your dear friend. You call him and agree to meet him tomorrow morning in a coffee shop. You meet him the next day for two hours of enjoyable conversation. This is a natural happening in reality: you have a desire, and you fulfill it in reality through actions. You fulfill your desire by meeting your friend. In this way you were creating your reality for a specific moment in the morning. But, what if you hadn't met your friend, because he had an emergency meeting at work? The outcome of this last-minute occurrence is that you tried to create a reality according to your desire and it didn't happen in the end. Therefore, we can understand from this example that you influence reality from your side and there are external factors that are influencing it too. In this example, that external factor was only the way your friend spent his free time.

It's only a simple and specific case but when we are dealing with life in general, this case represents the creation of reality.

Back to the example, let's make another scenario: in spite of your friend's cancellation, you decide to go to the coffee-shop, and enjoy a relaxing morning with a book. As you are sitting there, you notice one of your big customers sitting at the table next to you. You ask him to join you. You start with small talk that leads to closing a big business deal. So, what happened here? Was it only a simple coincidence? I call it magic: the way things fall into place in reality, and the good news is that the magic in your life works according to your deep desire. When you're unaware in life, this happening seems like a coincidence but when you are deeply aware of your life you can see the magic in action, you see how you are creating your reality. In this example, it was a meeting that was one piece of a larger puzzle. This puzzle is the desire that you summoned in a specific area of life. You didn't necessarily summon this exact meeting but you summoned a complex reality that this meeting is a part of creating.

This example is just a simple case study; it emphasizes the explanation only for a specific time. In life, it's happening in a more complicated way because of the huge amount of events and the fact that they are being created over a life time. As you can understand, the creation of reality doesn't work like we are used to in our physical reality, in which case, we summon and it works directly. The creation of reality works differently. It's based on other rules, conditions and language. It is an immeasurable, abstract process, which means that we can't observe the causes of the creation directly and that's the reason we're so unaware of it. In this chapter we will shed light on it to make it clearer. It's a process of understanding that takes a lifetime. Here we will focus the on the practical part.

Just to be clear, the creation of reality is not like pushing a button, and abracadabra, things happen! It's expressing your desire through decision and then implementing it with actions. I mention this not to be cynical but to avoid people being caught by an unbalanced spiritual attitude that minimizes the importance of taking actions in the physical world. I've been there. Creating reality must happen by balancing common sense decisions with actions that reflect one's inner world. When creating reality, harmony must exist to balance all the factors that influence reality.

Find the magic in life to create your reality

In order to use the magic of creation for practical uses, let's find out the essence of it in logical expressions, for the purpose of coping with common sense doubts.

We are acting in a physical world, we know things that we can see, smell, sense, hear and taste-- which means we know things that we can grasp with our 5 senses. For example, you can believe in aliens but you can't know their existence for sure because you haven't seen them with your own eyes, you've only heard about them. Therefore you can only believe or not believe in them but you can't know for sure; you know what the taste of tomato will be before eating it because you've already tasted it. You don't have to believe in what it will taste like because you've already tried it in the past, with your senses. The point here is that you know things if you've experienced them with at least one of your 5 senses.

There are facts you know, even without testing them directly with your 5 senses, only by seeing the outcome of their influence.

For example: gravity. Although you can't grasp gravity with your senses you just know it exists. It's enough for you to see the outcome of gravity (things are falling to the ground) and learn about it in order to know it.

In this chapter, I propose the same for you: to believe so much in your ability to create your reality, until you come to know it by trying it and then experiencing the outcome, although without ever grasping anything directly with your senses.   It's a challenge but it's worth it.

We are creators of our reality

We are creators; we are creating our reality in every moment of our life. We've forgotten how to do it according to our desires. This part of the Guide is a reminder for you of how to create your reality according to your vision. The way to do it is by summoning your reality.

Whenever I succeed in being aware of the influence of summoning my goals in reality and watch it happen, working for me like magic, I'm amazed at the magnificence of the creation of our life. It's almost impossible to believe because we live in a reality that is explained by scientific rules. That's the reason I developed a model: to discover how it can be that events happen in reality with a sense of magic. I wanted to explore how creating our reality is a natural ability. I know that it's hard to believe but the more you recreate your reality the more it will be natural for you.

Usually at this point most people react with doubts based on questions like, "How can it be? I've experienced life differently." This happens only because they haven't experienced their ability to create reality, or experienced it without being aware of it.

Now you have the opportunity to experience creation with awareness and then decide if it's true that you are creating your reality.

According to this attitude, this book is part of your summoning of reality, it's one of many stages on your path of life that you created by expressing your desires. Can you see it?

Do your magic: summon your reality

You are in the exact moment of recreating your reality. To make it happen you have to connect to your deep essence.

Just to be accurate, the use of 're' in recreating is to emphasize that reality is created over a life time by recreating it in every moment.

The feelings in the moment of summoning reality is like booking a vacation, ordering a new car, signing a contract for buying a new house, or signing a contract as an employee; they are all actions that are creating a future outcome. You can feel the excitement of expectation for the desired outcome that you longed for. You are in the same stage right now: you can "order" the goal by summoning your reality, so you have all the reasons to be excited for it!

For recreating your reality according to your goal, you have to use your ability to summon. It's expressing your desire for reality, so loudly that reality changes in accordance with your expression. It's like seeing a child that so deeply wants a new toy that you can see the whole of him expressing his desire to get it. Here you are like the child that wants something, and you ask reality to create it for you, only because you are expressing your desire.

Guided tools for creating your reality

Here, I propose to you to choose between two powerful tools that will guide you to summon your reality. I suggest that you read them both and decide which tool you want to use, they have the same purpose but apply different methods. Choose the one that attracts you more, you can choose them both but please do at least one of them, and only once. Repeating the process would raise doubts.

Guided tool for creating your reality (first tool)

Follow the instructions: they're a reminder to your essence of how to create reality. Just let these words guide you during the process:

Step 1:

Find your focus using the "Step-by-step tool to find your focus" that was presented to you in the beginning of this book. If you need to, go back to those instructions and follow them.

Step 2:

Go back to your desires, which you wrote in the chapter "Realize your Desire about the Chosen Area of Life" and re-read them, absorb them.

Step 3:

Think about the goal as a gate you want to cross through, beyond it you know that you have fulfilled your goal.

Step 4:

See in your mind the process that you will have to go through to fulfill the goal, you don't know exactly how you will cross, you only have a clue about it. Like an athlete standing on the starting line, he (or she) doesn't know exactly how each step or moment will be but they have an idea of what's waiting for them, they already know the track that they have to run on to finish the marathon. They've already done all the preparation and are ready for the race, and they're focusing on the route that they are going to take until they reach the finish line, a route that is paved for them to cross.

In your marathon, to reach the destination you have the path that you can follow. Now, in the moment before taking the first step, you are physically on the starting line but your mind can 'jump' into the core of the journey and continue to the destination. Therefore, you can experience the outcome of the goal as if it already happened.

See it, see yourself traveling along the path until you reach the goal. It may only be one moment of seeing flashes of your path to the goal, experience it happening right now, feel the feelings, be excited, and happy, with your achievement.

Keep from now on that feeling of excitement from knowing about the fulfillment of the goal, you 'signed the contract to order it'. The feelings are like Christmas; you have all the reason to celebrate and you feel that the entire world around you is smiling at you.

Decide if you want to do the second tool, as mentioned, it's an option.

Step-by step to summon your reality of the goal (second tool)
First read it all then do each step:

Step 1:
Find your focus using the "Step-by-step tool to find your focus" that was presented to you in the beginning of this book. If you need to, go back to those instructions and follow them.

Step 2:
Go back to the table that you prepared in the chapter "Discover your vision." The content of the table will help you in the next step.

Step 3:
Activate your imagination and take your mind to the future: pick a moment in which the goal has been fulfilled. It's a moment when you are already living in a routine after you have reached the destination.
(If you have problems imagining the goal in your mind, you can use the pictures/images that you made for the inspiration board. If you didn't prepare it, just find pictures on the internet or in magazines that visualize your goal and that make your feel inspiration towards the goal. Continue with the instructions with these pictures).
Write about this moment. Be as detailed and specific as you can. Describe it as a live event that's happening right now.

Examples for step 3 (for 4 different goals):
"I'm in a meeting with the stuff, hardly believe that it's a meeting of the start-up company that I founded, making plans based on the funding that we raised, feelings of hope and new beginnings are in the air, we are discussing the possibilities of marketing our product." A moment while fulfilling the goal: to found start-up company.

"I'm at my first exhibition of my paintings, a lot of people arrived, and come to hug, kiss and congratulate me, and a lot of interest about my work, I'm feeling so blessed and satisfied, finally my dream is coming true, even my parents are here." A moment while fulfilling the goal: to be an artist as a career.

"I'm entering the office of my new job, every one smiling at me with a morning greeting, I'm happy to start to work here, especially happy with my new salary, finally I'm getting paid for my efforts!" A moment while fulfilling the goal: a new job with a higher salary.

"I'm excited to begin writing the last chapter of my book, it is promising, and I have a feeling that it will be a best seller. The words just flow out from me; I'm expressing myself onto the paper. I'm inspired and feel satisfaction; I understand what the meaning of freedom is." A moment while fulfilling the goal: to be a writer as a career.

Step 4:
Renew your personality profile: Describe your new personality after you've reached the destination including state of mind, feelings, skills and abilities. Use details as much as you can.
Example: I feel confident to make decisions, I'm organized with my tasks, I manage my time wisely, I enjoy the freedom of making my own decisions, I feel satisfaction and pride with myself.

Step 5:
Bless the creation and thank yourself about it. Write and say it: words have the power of creating.   You can use the words:
"I bless the creation of _____(your goal) and thank myself for choosing it."

Step 6:

Let go!

Which means that you have finished the process of summoning your reality; treat it as something that you know; therefore, you don't have to believe any longer that it will happen because you know it will happen.

To make the switch from believing to knowing, do the following: describe again the moment that you chose in the last step, but, as if it already happened. Write your experiences in the past tense, describing it as a past event. Do it like you are telling your experiences of an exciting past event.

Examples for step 6 (for 4 different goals):

"It was such an important meeting, historical. The entire team met, planning out the investment that we raised. You could feel the excitement in the air. We have great people; I love them and everyone is talented. We were discussing the possibilities of marketing our product." The goal: to found a start-up company.

"It was a wonderful evening, I'll never forget it. A lot of important people were there and I was the center of attention. To see my name all over the room was exciting; I felt like a princess at her wedding! It was dream come true." The goal: to be an artist as a career.

"I started a new job. Finally, I found it. It's the same position but in a new company, and most importantly -- better money. It took me a long time to find it but I'm satisfied with it." The goal: a new job with a higher salary.

"I got a phone call from my publishing company. The CEO himself called me. He wanted the honor of reporting to me that the sales in the first quarter were very high, and even beyond expectations. He wanted to tell me directly that he believed in me from the first meeting and he is happy that they are working with me. I was in shock. I'm still digesting it. Let's go celebrate, drinks on me!" The goal: to be a writer as a career.

When you are ready, continue with the next chapter.

Chapter 14:
Vision becomes reality

You're ready to make your vision into reality.

Although changes are part of life, it's not easy to initiate and implement changes in life. That's why you need strategy: to change habits from your present routine and start new ones. Every change can be implemented in life, it's only a matter of changing habits from your present routine. Deep changes in life behave like an aircraft carrier- when it has to go in a different direction, it takes time and effort to change the course, but the change finally happens. Every change, even the big ones start to take place from the first step and then another and another until the change happens. So let's start from the first step on the path that will lead you all the way to your goal.

The entire process that you have done until now prepared you for this moment: making your vision a reality.

Create your new routine by developing a strategy

Your life is still influenced by past processes that created the present routine, that which you want to change. Therefore you need to create a new routine that will allow you to take actions to reach your goal. As you probably know, life is full of challenges, especially when you want to make a change. That's why it's important to create a path that continues from this point all the way to the destination and keep moving despite the barriers along the way. For this purpose you need a strategy: it will help you to implement your actions in your daily life and cope with the barriers while doing that. This chapter will guide you on how to develop your strategy.

Planning out a strategy and using it in your life will help you to reflect your vision with your actions in reality. Which means to make sure you will achieve what you really want in your life.

Guidelines for your strategy

1. Gather information before actions and use your vision as a guide.

You need enough information to put you in a place where you can decide on the actions that you should take in order to make your vision come true according to your desire.

The information has to supply you with a description of reality, serving you to explore enough possibilities from which to choose the actions you will take.

2. Characterizing the goal as a target.

You need to characterize the goal as a target. The target setting process is like using navigation software (GPS based). Using the software requires you to input an unequivocal, clear, practical and operationally-sound destination. By using navigation software, you can get directions to any destination on the globe; the condition is only to input an exact address, which is translated into coordinates on the map, and only then can the system guide you. This is also the case when determining a personal goal in life. Formulating a precise definition, an 'exact address', will help you to reach it.

3. Time & Task Management (TTM).

Time and Task Management are usually related to office activity but if you want to make a change in your life, you have to be efficient with your time and your actions, and the best way to do this is to plan and manage it wisely.

The next 3 chapters will help you to implement these guidelines as a strategy of actions to fulfill your goal.   These chapters are preparations for the actions, and present a way of life which allows you to implement your actions toward the goal. These chapters are comprehensive and guide toward a deep awareness. Their purpose is not only for reaching your goal but are also life changing.

Chapter 15:
Gathering the right information before decision-making

Knowledge is power. We are living in a world of information, which means it's easy to explore information that could be practical and useful for you.

In this step, you will gather information that will put you in a position to make decisions. Information can help you to make better and more efficient decisions. It empowers you by supplying you more certainty in an uncertain world. It's creating a description of reality, serving you to explore as many possibilities as you need in order to choose from them what your actions will be.

Open yourself to the possibilities in your reality

Regarding the chosen area of life for change, you are on a path in that specific area of life and now you want to make a change, therefore you need to realize what the possibilities are in reality that can allow you to express this desire.

For example: A person suffering from acrophobia. He decides to make a change. He sets a goal to make his problem disappear. He opens himself to information on possibilities, reads about a variety of treatments and decides on using a method that was, until now, unheard of by him but has persuasive recommendations: NLP (Neuro-linguistic programming).

NLP is just an example and it doesn't mean that just because it's new for you, it's automatically better. The idea is to open your mind to a variety of possibilities and then objectively choose the right one for you.

Information provides you the freedom to choose

When you open yourself to a variety of possibilities, you have the freedom to choose the next actions. No matter what the area of life you want to change is, you need information about it before taking any action.

We are living in wonderful period of time with easy access to a huge amount of information. You can easily access information on any subject.

Use your common sense

When exploring information, it's important to remember that information is not an absolute truth. It's only information and when you are looking for information before actions it has to be treated as a recommendation and not as instructions for automatic implementation. You have to use awareness and common sense with it. This includes formal publications like articles about research. These are not necessarily scientific. You don't have any guarantee they're accurate for you. The same with informal information: it reflects other experiences and advice, and it's not necessarily your truth. Not everything is as black and white as it sometimes seems. Therefore, even the most recommended option, or option that was approved by researchers, doesn't automatically fit your life. You have to examine it first and use your common sense. If necessary, get advice from professionals or someone else that you trust. This is also part of the process of gathering information and then making a decision about it.

All this is written not to make you suspicious but only to expand your awareness and sharpen your focus and allow you to use information for your own benefit. At the end of the day, they're your decisions on your life.

The "funnel method"

The method that I use for gathering information and arriving at useful knowledge is the "funnel method". This method can allow you to take advantage of the huge amount of information that's accessible to you and then create the necessary focus for deciding on actions.

It is a method that I used as a Social Science researcher and integrated it as a tool that can help me to deal with a large amount of information. When exploring information as a basis for actions, like the process that you are doing right now, the information has to go from general to narrow branches in order to supply the focus that you need for your actions.

This method is offered to you to first explore a wide range of information and then narrow it down according to your preferences until you focus on the information that is the perfect match to your vision. Begin by creating topics and then drill down into each of these topics, exploring them on a deeper level. This way every topic creates one or more branches of information that you can choose from. With this method, you will be free to choose from many possibilities that are good fits for you. It's much simpler than it may sound. Keep reading for examples and instructions.

Example one: You are feeling bored with your routine and decide to do something about it. You are gathering information on activities to do in your leisure time. You are looking for an activity that will be enjoyable and interesting. You decide to narrow the search down to three activities that seem attractive to you: learning Spanish, building a robot, taking a fencing course. You continue the search for information on each of these, as separate branches, and then you decide on one of them.

As you can see, the purpose of gathering information is to understand what your choices are in your present reality- gathering information is the description of the choices in your reality. In the example, it was the various hobbies that you could choose from.

This information is the base of the choices that you decide from. You start from general information about your desire and then focus it by creating branches of information.

Example two: you set a goal to improve your experience of parenthood. The destination point is clear but you haven't decided on how to do it. First you gather information about parenthood and then you filter down the information, which leads you to knowledge about the choices that attracted you on ways of life, methods, and attitudes for better parenthood. The choice you make will act as the base for the actions you will take to fulfill your goal.

Example three: you decide to improve your wellbeing. You are gathering information about it, starting with information about health and wellbeing in general. You screen articles, blogs, research, posts, recommendations, tips and the experiences of others. You expose yourself to a variety of information about it. You decide that sports activities, nutrition, taking up a new hobby and meditation are the most promising choices for you. Therefore, you focus on information about them and then decide which to pursue out of them. Of course, when you decide, don't choose more than you are actually capable of committing to.

Choose your source of information
The internet is a source of information, but not the only one. There are other sources, like talking with others, going to lectures or workshops, meeting in groups, etc. The most important thing in gathering information is observation of reality in the present and staying open to all options.

A practical process of gathering information according to the "funnel method"

1. Explore the subject in general by: using a search engine on the web; talking about it with people (at work, your close circle, etc.); joining groups; listening to lectures; subscribing to newsletters; and/or watching webinars or courses on the internet.

As you explore the information, write comments in your notebook:

a. I have to remember that....

b. I think the best thing for me is.....

c. It's interesting that.....

d. Et cetera

2. Focus on the information by using the vision table that you made in the chapter "Discover Your Vision". Each row of the table has three columns. You have to find the choices that reflect the first column ("Things that concern you in the present") and allow you to make the content in the second column ("Your vision") come true and make you feel the content in third column ("Feelings"). You don't have to match up each item in the table exactly with the information you're gathering, but use the table as a guideline for the information that will lead you to the right choices.

Example:

Area of life that has to be changed: **career.**

Things that concern you in the present:	The best idea to solve your concern	Inner Changes
Lack of free time	A job with less hours	Freedom
Emptiness	Find what makes me feel fulfilled	Fulfilled
I find myself getting bored frequently	A challenging job that will be dynamic	Interesting
I get tired from driving every day in traffic	Work somewhere closer or consider working from home	Comfortable
Low salary	Well-paid job- I'm worth it	Satisfied

When you are exploring the information about career, you want to find information about career that will reply to the first column, allow you to make true the content in the second column ("Your vision") and make you feel the content in third column ("Feelings").

Chapter 16:
Characterizing the goal as a target

Every goal needs to be a practical target that will help you to focus your efforts in order to fulfill the goal.

Read the following guide on how to define the goal with examples and then write your goal according to it:

Step 1: Make a clear, practical and operational definition.
The goal has to include a destination that must be easy to understand and practical to reach;
It's like setting a destination in navigation software- you can't set North as a destination but only an exact address.

For example:
"My goal is to have a career change." This is like setting North as a destination.
This is an abstract destination that can't be measured or defined. It's a good start --you're expressing a wish to start moving-- but it's not complete quite yet because there isn't a clear, feasible objective that could be reached by taking steps.

"My goal is to work from home, four hours a day, in online marketing, making $90,000/year."
This is a good example for determining a clear, measurable, practical and operationally-sound goal. You can figure out exactly how to get there. In addition, there is a reasonable chance that you can reach it even if you are currently an employee and you don't know (yet) how you'll do it.

Step 2: Set a timeframe.
Part of the target is the timeframe, you don't want it to slowly get lost and fade away during the day-to-day bustle. Therefore you need to set this timeframe.

To set the time frame, answer the question: what is the end point of the actions that you have to take in order to reach the goal?

The answer has to include your wishing to reach it as fast as you can and also a realistic understanding of the actions and efforts that you need to take in order to fulfill the goal, which is the point that when you cross it, you know that you've reached your goal. At this point, it's only an estimate using the knowledge that you have now. Don't worry about being 100% accurate right now. Just make an assumption even if it's new to you.

If your goal falls outside of the one year timeframe, try reframing it in steps. For example, if you had set the goal 'get my Ph.D. in 3 years,' you could reframe it to Step 1: 'finish my proposal for the research committees within 6 months', and so on.

Step 3: Write the goal on a new page in your notebook with bold letters.

My goal is_____

Congratulations, you have set a new goal!

When you are ready, continue with the next chapter.

Chapter 17:
Time and Task Management

Time and Task Management (TTM) is the way to turn your vision into an action that you can implement immediately in your daily life. It's a very efficient way to live life in general: to make the most out of time and allow you prioritize your actions in life.

I know that some may recoil from TTM, because it sounds official and technical, but in fact this is an efficient method to make the best out of your precious time and make your decisions to take actions.

TTM doesn't have to be official or hard to implement. In the following chapter, you'll have the chance to learn and use the light and easy version of TTM. You can use it not only for your goals but also for your other activities.

TTM can help you to:

1. Set new priorities.
When you realize what your desire is and you're willing to implement it in your reality as a goal, you become more aware and able to decide on new priorities in your life. Time and Task Management helps you to make new priorities happen.

2. Make the best use of your time.
As you probably know, time flies. When you're efficient with your time, you can get the most out of time in order to achieve what is important to you in your life.

3. Keep going in the right direction.
Life can pull you in many directions; you need direction for your goal, like a compass, in order to keep on track with the goal while still being flexible with the challenges.

4. Implement the changes gradually and in a balanced way.
The way to control the process --and also experience and enjoy it-- can be by initiating the change gradually and in a balanced way instead of trying to do everything at once. That's why it's important to work with TTM- it's a long-term plan of actions, and is implemented one step at a time.

5. Be persistent.
The power of persistence can be learned from water. The never-ending flow makes it one of the major forces that design our planet: it can shape any material in nature. It flows through mountains, rocks, earth. It continues no matter the barrier. Sometimes it changes course to pass obstacles but always continues on until it reaches its final destination. Nothing can stop it. You can be the same way: using TTM to continue taking actions until reaching your destination.

Time Management
In time management, you decide on the priorities of your time. You need Time Management because your time is full of activities that belong to your 'old world', and now you want to make a change, so you need to find the time to do it. There is a range of how tightly you can manage your time. Here, the suggestion is light management, which is only to make the outline of your new routine. Time Management is important for every goal, even for emotional ones like finding one's significant other; these take time like any other, so you have to find this time to work on them.

Schedule now in your calendar regular daily (or weekly) time to do the activities until reaching the goal. If your start day is tomorrow, the end of the timeframe is according to your decision about how long it will take to fulfill the goal. The duration of each activity should be at least one hour, depending, of course, on your goal and your ability to make time for it.

Examples:
Timeframe: July 5th-Oct.5th. Every day from 9-10pm.
Timeframe: July 8th-Aug.8th. Every Monday and Wednesday: 8-10pm.
If you are an employee in a company, the time would be during your free time from work, which means early morning or evening; as a self-employed person, you can do it during the day, based on your decision about what the time is for it.
If you can't commit to a regular time in your schedule, try to commit to a minimum of hours every week to fulfill your goals.

I know that probably you don't have free time but you have to remember that time is made of priorities, and I think that your goal becomes top priority, that is the reason for time management, to reorganize your time according to the change you want to implement in your life.

Task Management
Task Management is the most efficient method to plan and manage your actions in a timeframe in order to achieve your goals. For planning and managing your tasks with Task Management, you don't need any experience or professional knowledge in Project Management but only common sense.
The key for Task Management is to decide what actions will reflect your vision- it's expressing yourself in reality. The information that you gathered will help you to decide what the right actions will be. There are no mistakes in Task Management because there isn't

only one path to fulfill your goal, but many. That's the reason for making decisions; you make your path by making a decision about one task out of many options and each time take one step until you reach your destination. Here, in this stage, you'll be guided to make these decisions.

During your planning and doing according Task Management, please remember that it's not a scientific method. You just estimate and plan as best you can according to your knowledge in the present. It's for yourself, just to make sure that things will happen according to your vision.
You can use different methods and tools for managing tasks. There are plenty of tools and methods that are being offered online. I use only a simple To Do list.

Preparation before planning your tasks:
1. Throughout the entire process of Task Management, use the 'Discover your vision' and 'Use fears to motivate and to navigate' chapters as guidelines. This means use them as guidelines to plan and do your activities and also use them every time you have a dilemma, bump into an obstacle, or feel confused or helpless.
2. Review the information that you wrote during the chapter 'Gathering the right information before decisions'. This will be the basis for your decisions during the task planning.

The tools for Task Management:
Quick tasks: tasks that can be done all at once, which means tasks that are started and finished on the same occasion, like sending an email, call someone, or scheduling a meeting.
You can use the following simple table. It's only for planning the tasks and then making sure that they get done. It's better to set time aside to do them, if you can ('Scheduled time' on table).

Task	Scheduled time	Done?

Long-term tasks: there are two types of tasks.

1. Tasks which can't be done all at once because their made up of short tasks, for example, meeting investors for my planned start-up company.

2. Tasks which have to be done gradually, for example, quitting smoking as a part of changing habits.

You can use the following simple table. It's for planning the tasks, estimated start time and estimated time to accomplish them.

Task	Start Time	Estimated time you need to accomplish the task	Done?

The amount of detail depends on your attitude: how much you want to focus the process of planning the tasks. If you want, you can plan them as only a list of to-do tasks without a timeframe.

Sub-goals

Sub-goals allow you to manage the path as milestones until you reach your destination. This will give you better control over your progress.

The sub-goals can be fulfilled one goal at a time - which means reaching one sub-goal and then the next (linear method) or fulfilling the sub-goals parallel to each other (parallel method).

First example - the goal: find a new job.
First sub-goal: write resume and send it to 10 companies.
Second sub-goal: do interviews with 10 companies.

Second example -the goal: better well-being.
First sub-goal: improve nutrition.
Second sub-goal: stop smoking.
Third sub-goal: keep doing a sports activity once a week.
Fourth sub-goal: start a new hobby.

The first example has to be done according to the linear method: you first write your resume and send it and only then can you do the interviews.
In the second example, you can choose if you want to fulfill the sub-goals according to the linear method or according to the parallel method; it's up to you.

Splitting your goal into sub-goals allows you not only to manage your tasks better but also to experience satisfaction along the way. Each sub-goal is like a goal itself: it's a big achievement.
You can use the following simple table for planning the sub-goals, including estimated time to accomplish them.

Sub-goal	Estimated time you need to accomplish the sub-goal

To implement Task Management in your life, do the following:
Full example will follow these instructions.

Step 1: Set sub-goals.
Split your goal into sub-goals. Write it as a list or a one-column table. In this stage, you can just make an educated guess about what the sub-goals are.

Use the information you gathered in the chapter 'Gathering the right information before decisions'. Decide if you need further information to set the sub-goals. Please remember that you are at the beginning of your path; you don't know everything yet, plan according to your present knowledge, and know you'll have the chance to update it later.

Decide which method you'll use to fulfill sub-goals: linear method or parallel method. It depends on the goal, your ability and your time.

Step 2: Split each sub-goal into tasks.
Plan out the tasks that you have to do in order to fulfill the sub-goals. They can be quick tasks or long-term tasks.

Step 3: Split long-term tasks (if you have them) into quick tasks.

Step 4: Prepare a time table for sub-goals.

Estimate as best you can a realistic time to reach every sub-goal. It's for preparing yourself to do it, and also for committing to yourself. Now it's only an educated guess and maybe you're not used to evaluating time for doing your tasks. In this stage, it's only a timeframe to focus your progress towards the goal. Estimate your sub-goals as best you can now. It's a practice, the more you experience practicing planning and estimating time for your sub-goals, the more accurate you'll become.

Step 5: Scheduled time to manage this plan.

Set in your schedule a weekly time (10 minutes each time) for maintaining this plan: 1. check if you've done the planned tasks 2. decide if you need to change the planned tasks and to plan new tasks. 3. Check your progress.

The time to do this could be the time that you set in time management, or some other time.

Execute the tasks

Do these tasks in your daily life; implement them in your reality in the time that you set in Time Management. It's important to keep continuing to act and keep moving according to your plan.

Example for Task Management:

A person decides to improve his well-being as a goal. His vision is to feel good with himself, to live a healthy life, to have an athletic look, and to enjoy life. While gathering information he explored information about ways to do it. He decided on 4 sub-goals: 1. Improve nutrition. 2. Stop smoking. 3. Do a sports activity once a week. 4. Find a hobby.

Tasks for accomplishing the sub-goal: improve nutrition

Task	Done?
Eat less sugar	
Make weekly order of organic vegetables from organic farm	
Call Casey and ask for her recipe for healthy soup that she was telling me about	
Subscribe to magazine "Eat Healthy"	
Find solution for emotional eating	

There are tasks that may take longer to accomplish like finding a solution for emotional eating, and eating less sugar, therefore he sets them each as long-term tasks that are made up of short, daily tasks.

Long-term task: eat less sugar

Task	Done?
Drink coffee without sugar	
Eat less sugary cakes	
Drink less sugary drinks	
Eat less chocolate	

After he summarizes the tasks that he has to do, he estimates the time to accomplish these sub-goals.

It can be in parallel ('parallel method') or by doing them one after another ('linear method'), depending on his ability and his desire to fulfill the goal.

Time table for Sub-goals:

Sub-goal	Time to start	time to accomplish	Done?
Stop smoking	May 1	May 31	
Start doing a sports activity once a week	May 1	-	
Start better nutrition	June 1	-	

As you can see, some of his sub-goals use the parallel method while another is linear.

When you are ready, continue with the next chapter.

Chapter 18: Letting go

As a child, it was easy for me to let go of events that happened. It was natural to be naïve and to trust the world around me with the belief that events happened for a good reason. But over time, negative feelings began to accumulate and leave their mark with an untrusting attitude towards the world. The outcome was difficulties letting go.

Letting go was the last part of my journey of awareness. It took me a while to realize the meaning of letting go and how to "learn" something that should be so natural in life.

Letting go is an attitude for how to react to the uncertain in life, which usually causes us to want to take control of our lives. In this chapter, we'll understand the meaning of letting go in life. We'll also find the balance between letting go and taking control of life.

Up until this stage you are taking control of your life by setting goals and starting to implement them in your life through actions. Now, it's time to integrate the 'letting go'.

Why is it important to let go?
1. **To enjoy life**.
When you let go, you can enjoy your activities. It's valid for every action: when you release your control and let go of emotions and feelings, you can enjoy any activity. It works according to this rule: the more your actions are new experiences for you, the more feelings of fears and excitement will arise, and the more you let these feelings arise, the more you will enjoy the actions.
Let's take a radical example using an extreme activity like bungee-jumping, why do it if it's dangerous? For the adrenaline? Why does

it create adrenaline? Because you lose control for few seconds and then suddenly a new experience is happening and in those moments, excitement mixed with fear creates complete enjoyment. I haven't tried bungee-jumping and I'm not planning on it because it's much easier to enjoy everyday moments of life, just by trying new experiences as much as possible, and by making new decisions. In this process you are doing just that- by making decisions about a new goal. You take yourself on new experiences so don't forget to allow yourself to let go to enjoy the journey.

2. To experience your deep essence.

When you let go you can experience your deep essence, your being. In that way you evolve. The evolvement works like this: you react to the events that you summoned because part of you desired them and worked towards them by setting goals. These events come in unexpected packaging and when you get them you have to let go, release control and expectation, and enjoy and experience the feelings that arise- it's the part inside of you that desired this event in the first place. These desires could be for example: an independent life, being in love, being creative, being in abundance, or even being silly for one day. It could be anything at all, anything you desire or wish for. These desires help you to experience your being. This is the cycle of creation with you as creator.

Letting go and accepting the upcoming

1. Letting go: accept the uncertain while hoping for the best.

Here are some examples of different scenarios that could happen:

a. You arrive to work Monday morning and you're just walking through the door to your office and you find that your desk has disappeared.

b. Your boss calls you for a private meeting.

c. You see five missed calls from someone that you love.

d. You get a phone call from your mother that begins with "don't ask, I'm in shock....".

These are dramatic moments with unknown outcomes. You could easily misinterpret any one of them as negative events and react hastily.

Before you begin to panic, if you let go and allow events to happen and accept reality as it is then you may find that the upcoming events are positive.

To continue to a happy ending:

a. You get to work and you find out that your table disappeared because you are getting a new one.

b. Your boss is calling you to a private meeting to announce you've been given a raise.

c. You are seeing 5 missed calls from someone that you love because he needs help with his car.

d. You are getting a phone call from your mother saying "don't ask, I'm in shock... we won the lottery."

Sometimes there isn't a happy ending. We will discuss this in the next section.

2. Letting go: accepting the unexpected.
Examples:
a. You enter your hotel room and you find out that the room is not the one you booked.
b. You decided to start learning Spanish and your teacher is doesn't show up to the first lesson.
c. You are on a blind date and your date is not like your friend described.
These are all situations that can happen; you expected one outcome and get another. The perfect thing about life is that every moment is a new opportunity, like a new hand of cards. Maybe this round you have lousy cards but the next round may be different. The key for coping with unwanted reality is first to accept it and then decide what to do next.

Moving forward with the previous examples:
a. You enter the hotel room...then you go to the manager and he gives you his best suite.
b. The Spanish teacher didn't show up.... In the spare time you go to a coffee shop and run into a friend that you hadn't seen since high school.
c. You are on a blind date.... After a long conversation, you decided instead to explore the possibility of starting a new business together.

But sometimes events end up being less desirable
Eventually things work out. In reality, a desirable event doesn't necessarily follow an undesirable one, sometimes you have to wait longer until good things arrive, but in the long term, you have to remember that things always work out. You can look back at the past and see that every crisis that was in the past was settled one way or another. When happening, things that work out in

unexpected ways make us believe in luck, destiny, coincidence, etc. It makes sense because we don't have logical explanations for such occurrences. But in fact, when we look at life with a macro view, we can see patterns and notice that we are controlling our life in the long run.

In the long term, events in reality happen according your vision. This is one of the reasons for discovering your vision: to control your life, to make sure that the events that happen will be as you desire. But in the short term, you can't know what the events will be exactly; you can only believe that present events will somehow fit into your grand plan.

The balance between letting go and taking control of your life is having goals

On the surface it may seem that letting go is the opposite of taking control but in fact they complete one another and give you a full life. I learned that when looking on our life with a macro view, we can see that we have desires that motivate us to achieve goals. We can choose to take control of our lives to achieve our goals, but as we move towards the goal, we need to let events happen in order to experience and enjoy life.

It's the same process that you're going through now.

How to?
1. Letting go by being in a relationship with reality.

Like in any relationship, there's a mutual give and take: one side is giving and the other is taking, and vice versa. The type of giving and taking changes according to the type of relationship.

When you're in a relationship with reality, you give by expressing yourself through actions, and you take by letting go and accepting the outcome of reality. In fact, this relationship is being implemented now during this process that this book is guiding you through. This chapter deals with the side of taking, which happens by letting go and accepting reality.

2. Believe in yourself. Let go and just believe in yourself.

Letting go is believing in yourself because you know you've done your best with the best intentions, and therefore after your actions, you can only expect the best. You can let go and just believe in yourself. You know that every moment you're free to decide what will be because you know that you are the creator of your life.

When you are taking control of your life you can easily let go and you can change the 'taking control' mindset to trusting in yourself that you're doing the best, and placing that same trust on reality, which means to be in a relationship with reality. You know that only the right events will happen. You worked on your beliefs in the chapter 'Empower your self-belief'. Whenever you feel difficulties with letting go, work with your beliefs. This will empower your sense of control over life, which in turn empowers you to let go.

3. Letting go by forgiveness.

The things that are difficult to let go of are all those things you try to grab, hang on to, cope with, resist, or regret. The difficulty in letting go comes from the fact that painful events have a deep influence on your present life. To let go of these emotions, you have to forgive. You forgive yourself and also others. Forgiveness is extremely powerful and sometimes when the pain is too much, it's hard to let go and forgive. But you have to let go, in order to move on.

So, now you can let go, experience your being and enjoy life. You deserve it.

When you're ready, move on to the next chapter.

Chapter 19:
What if something goes wrong?

On your way to your goal, things may happen that don't align with it: undesired outcomes happen in reality -- you bump into a problem and you have negative feelings that cause a loss of motivation and bother you -- or any other barrier that reduces or stops your efforts towards the goal.

Whenever it seems to you that something goes wrong, before reacting to it, follow these steps.

First, please remember that there are no mistakes or wrong actions.
There are no mistakes, but just your decisions and actions: every outcome is created for a reason. If you realize that something seems wrong, there is no need to fix, or regret what's done. It's already past; accept the outcome and decide what to do next. Remember that in every moment you can change your reality and make another decision and change the course of your movement; just slightly shift direction, while using the vision as a compass to keep on track to the destination.

Then,
Lift your head, look out on the horizon and see the journey that you have to go on until reaching the goal that was created from milestones. When you arrive to another milestone, you know that after you've passed it, you've gotten closer to your goal.
This entire journey that you are taking now is a process of narrowing gaps between the undesired reality and your desires. Every barrier is just a trace from the old reality that you need to change in order to create your new and desired reality.

Another thing,
You had such challenges before and you overcame them. You prepare for any challenge that comes in your path. If fact, challenges are created for your experience, even the hard ones.

Therefore,
Every time you bump into a barrier, you can see it as a challenging riddle on your adventure that you have to solve; you can trust yourself, knowing that there is solution for it and you just have to find it, and when you do, you will be one step closer towards the goal. You will also feel satisfied and proud of yourself. This is the essence of fulfilling goals.

How to
In the case of a reduction or halt in your progress, do the following:
1. **Don't worry**, things can happen.
2. **Accept** the reality as it is. Don't resist or regret it.
3. **Diagnose and understand** the source of the problem: awareness brings with it the solution. Ask questions about the situation: What's wrong? What caused it to happen? Why has it stopped my progress?
4. **Change your attitude in your inner world**: use the tools in this book. Skim the chapters and pick the tools that you need to make changes in your inner world: to cope with fears; loss of beliefs; loss of passion; confusion; loss of confidence, etc. Just open the book, pick and read again the chapters that attract you and fit the issue. At least one of the chapters will be able to help. Reuse the chapters as tools for making the change.
5. **Change reality by taking another route**: assume the attitude of 'for any problem there is a solution'. Feel confident in yourself and find that solution to the problem, and according to the solution, make the decision that will change the situation at present and bring you back on track.

Make yourself another route:
a. Go back to the vision (your vision is your 'base camp').
b. Use the Task Management method (if you haven't used it yet, now is a perfect time to start) to re-plan your actions based on your vision according to the present. Now you have more information and you can change your plan's tasks and decide on the change(s) that you have to do. It means that you, at this point, have to evolve in order to fulfill your goal and to decide on a new path to make it happen.
You can imagine reaching a new obstacle that seems, on first impression, like a wall. But if you see it as a challenge that you can cope with, you will activate your creativity and improve your ability to get over that wall. This is the evolvement process. Without obstacles, there wouldn't be evolvement.
In any case, keep moving and make decisions to change the present, knowing that you have all that you need inside of you, and you are prepared for coping with any situation.
d. Open yourself to new possibilities: during your new route, open yourself to new possibilities when you are making decisions. Be creative with your decisions, do things differently and try new things.
e. You are the commander of the process: it all depends on your decisions, make the decision of what to do next.
f. Be dynamic: don't stop, there is always another possibility, you just need to find it. Make new decisions based on the present reality, which you have in one hand, with your vision in the other.

When you are ready, continue with the next chapter.

Chapter 20: What's next?

Keep taking actions with your vision as a guide until you reach your goal (if you didn't do the first step, now is a perfect time to do that).

Keep the balance in your life

Keep the balance in your life, don't initiate hasty actions, take one step at the time. This means starting to initiate a gradual change while continuing with your present routine. For example, do not leave your day job in the first step (career). Sometimes, the desire can cause us to make a quick change but please don't rush the process- although it's important to make decisions and act, it's even more important to do it gradually and with balance.

Between your desires and your goals – your life

By having reached this stage in your journey, it means you have listened to your desire and are making changes in your life that are moving you forward. The more goals you set, the fuller your life will be.

When you are ready (it can be parallel to this goal) decide on a new goal, and implement it with this Guide, this time it will be faster.

Enjoy life

Remember to enjoy everything along the way; that's the meaning of life. It's all happening for you, to enjoy and experience during your actions in reality. I'm sure that there will be things that stress you and put you under pressure, not only with this goal, but with other issues that may bother you. However, you can act while making the best out of any situation, being positive, doing your best and expecting great things to happen. As you probably understand by now, you are creating your reality. Choose the happy version of reality and happy will happen. It's a promise.